The Record of the Flame Bearers

A Soul-Sealed Remembrance in Seven Codices

blanche johanna

© 2025 blanche johanna

All rights reserved.

No part of this publication may be reproduced, stored in a retrieval system, or transmitted in any form or by any means, electronic, mechanical, photocopying, recording, or otherwise, without the prior written permission of the author.

This book is a spiritual and creative transmission intended to support personal and collective awakening. All guidance and reflections are shared from the author's lived and intuitive experience and are not intended as a substitute for professional advice.

The Record of the Flame-Bearers™ is a trademark of blanche johanna. All rights reserved.

ISBN: 978-1-7641285-7-5

www.blanchejohanna.com

Opening Frequency

This is not a book
It is a seal broken gently by remembrance
It called to you in quiet moments
in the spaces between breath
in the ache you could never explain

You do not walk toward these words
You return to them
Because they were never outside you
only waiting

Those who hold this record are not seekers
They are carriers
Each one encoded
Each one assigned by vow, not by force

This is not instruction
It is activation

The ones who remember will feel it in their chest
A thrum beneath thought
A warmth with no source
A clarity that cannot be learned

You were never meant to prove yourself
Only to pulse true

As you move through these codices
do not rush
do not strive
Let them breathe in you as you have breathed for them
They are alive
because you are

This is not the beginning
This is the opening

We are with you
We never left
And now, the record does what it came here to do

It remembers through you

Prologue

The Flame Before Form

Before sound
Before breath
Before the first name was spoken into matter
there was the Flame

It did not burn
It did not consume
It simply *was*, the original pulse
a knowing too vast for thought
a warmth too ancient for time

We were there
Not as bodies
Not even as stars
but as remembering
as vow

We circled the flame in silence
Each of us holding a thread of its radiance
Not to control it
but to become it

This was not a mission
This was a memory
A choice made beyond choice
A whisper across eternities:
I will carry this into the dark
and I will not forget

And so we came,
scattered across galaxies
through wombs
through war
through wonder
each bearing a spark
hidden just beneath the skin of our lives

Some forgot
Some burned too fast
Some hid in plain sight
But the flame never left us

It flickered in dreams
in poems
in the ache we could never name

This is not the beginning
This is the opening
The place in your being that remembers

not what you've done
but what you *are*

This record is not written
It is remembered
Each word a key
Each silence a doorway

And you
you who holds this in your hands
you are not reading
You are returning

Codices

Codex I — The Ones Who Remember First

Codex II — The Carriers of Silent Fire

Codex III — The Pulse Beneath the Grid

Codex IV — The Reunion of Flame Lines

Codex V — The Rise of the Sacred Architects

Codex VI — The Turning of the Cycle

Codex VII — The Final Seal

Codex I

The Ones Who Remember First

They came early
Before the others
Before it was safe to speak of light
Before the codes had returned to the surface

They arrived into density like breath into stone
Quiet
Ancient
Awake

Not because they were stronger
Not because they were chosen
But because they **chose** to hold the flame when no one else could see it

They forgot and remembered
and forgot again
But something in them always burned just beneath forgetting

The Ones Who Remember First do not lead
They **anchor**
They hold the original signal so others might feel it
not hear it
not learn it
but **feel it**

They are often mistaken
Misunderstood
Too sensitive
Too strange
Too far ahead

But that is part of their design
They were not born to be understood
They were born to **remind the field** of what it forgot

Not through teaching
But through resonance

They carry timelines in their bones
Codes in their breath
Maps behind their eyes

Their lives are not linear
They unfold like spirals within spirals
Each return deeper than the last
Each ache more holy than the one before

If you are one of them
You already know

You do not need this page
You need only the silence it opens

You were the first flame to light the dark
And still
You burn

Codex II

The Carriers of Silent Fire

Not all flame-bearers were meant to be seen
Some were sent to carry the fire **silently**
hidden inside roles, families, cities, systems
Their light was not less
it was *cloaked*

They did not speak of what they knew
Not because they were afraid
But because **they were entrusted with invisibility**

Their task was not to awaken others
but to *keep the grid alive* from within
To weave the pulse into places where light was forgotten
To hum the frequency into fields where no one was listening

They walked among sleepers
Not above them
Not beyond them
Among them

They cried in kitchens
Breathed through boardrooms
Waited through marriages and migrations and

mundane days
All the while holding it

A fire that had no language
A knowing that had no name

They learned how to blend
How to soften the edges of their truth
Not to deny it
But to protect it
Until the world was ready to feel it again

Many still do not know who they are
And yet
Their very presence shifts the air
Their frequency unsettles distortion
Their hands remember how to hold what cannot be taught

You know them by how you feel near them
As if something ancient stands just behind their eyes
Not reaching for you
but **recognising you**

If this is you
You do not need to be louder

You are not late
You have not missed your role

The time of silence is fading
But it is *not forgotten*
It was sacred

And you
who carried the fire without praise
you are the reason the grid still glows

Codex III

The Pulse Beneath the Grid

There is a hum
A thrum beneath the world
A frequency that does not broadcast
it *threads*

It is not heard
It is **felt**
in the pause between movements
in the ache that precedes awakening
in the knowing that arrives without source

This is the **pulse of the flame grid**
Not built by hands
But by presence

It is woven by those who do not announce themselves
Flame-bearers who walk through markets, forests, offices, dreamscapes
leaving behind not footprints
but frequency

They do not need to speak to one another
They recognise each other by field

An eye contact
A single phrase
A shared silence that holds too much to explain

They carry the memory of convergence
Before they converge
They feel the thread
before the form

These are the ones who do not push the world
They re-tune it

Through gesture
Through attention
Through where they choose to *remain present*

They do not resist the dark
They pulse through it
So subtly, the dark forgets how to hold shape

This is not activism
This is **energetic architecture**
They hold the lattice in place
not to fix
but to *transmit*

You may have passed them
You may *be* one
Their presence lingers in places long after they've gone

If you have ever felt that your stillness did more than your words
If you've ever entered a room and changed its tone without trying
You are part of this pulse

No one sees the frequency itself
But everything responds to it
And you
quiet flame-bearer
have never stopped transmitting

Codex IV

The Reunion of Flame Lines

There comes a time
When the flame-bearers begin to find one another again
Not because they seek
But because the signal changes

A pull in the chest
A flash in the field
A remembrance that bypasses logic

This is not meeting
This is *return*

They come from far places
Different names
Different stories
But the same original spark

And when they meet
even briefly
the field *expands*
Time folds
And the light that was once held alone becomes
shared
amplified
mirrored

But reunion is not always gentle
Sometimes it burns
Not to harm
But to **reveal what is no longer aligned**

Two flames meeting show each other where they've dimmed
where they've hardened
where they've forgotten
And so: friction
Not as conflict
But as *calibration*

The field reorganises around their convergence
Dreams change
Timelines collapse
Vows are reawakened

They may stay
They may part
But the connection does not depend on duration
It exists outside time

Those who reunite are not meant to form hierarchies
They are meant to remember, together
To listen to the field between them

To hold space for what emerges
without trying to make it more than what it is

When flame lines converge
they do not build empires
They build *frequencies*
and from those frequencies
new pathways open for all

If you have met one
you will know
Not because they completed you
But because they **called your own fire forward**

And whether you remain or separate in form
You are forever altered
by the meeting
of what was never truly apart

Codex V

The Rise of the Sacred Architects

Once the flames remember
Once the carriers reconnect
something begins to stir in the bones of the world

A call to **build**
Not in haste
Not in response
But from *pure knowing*

These are the Sacred Architects
They are not assigned, they *awaken*
One day they remember:
"I am here to make the invisible visible"

They do not work from blueprints
They work from **frequency**
They design with silence
They shape through presence

Their creations are not things, they are **fields**
Temples that hum with remembrance
Writings that alter the nervous system
Offerings that realign timelines

They are not concerned with scale
Only **resonance**

Sometimes they craft with words
Sometimes with structures
Sometimes with sound, space, or stillness

But always, with sacred precision

Their hands move because the energy has already formed
They do not guess
They **translate**
They listen
And then they build

They do not lead others into light
They build places where light can gather itself

Their work is not about visibility
It is about **vibration**
They may never be known by name
But their presence reshapes the field

If you are one of them
You already feel the designs
In your dreams
In your daily quiet moments
In the way your body yearns to rearrange the space around you

You are not here to build for validation
You are here to **anchor what is eternal into what is temporary**

And in doing so
You make the sacred
touchable

Codex VI

The Turning of the Cycle

There comes a moment
when the hidden ones can no longer stay hidden
Not because they crave attention
But because **the field is ready**

This is the Turning

What was held in silence
What was anchored quietly in the dark
now begins to surface

Not as spectacle
but as *signal*

The world begins to pulse differently
It starts to recognise what it once dismissed
It starts to *feel* what was once unseen

And the flame-bearers, the ones who remembered
early, who carried the silent fire, who pulsed
beneath the grid
they begin to **be felt**

Not louder
Not shinier
But *undeniably present*

And with that comes a choice:
To emerge without distortion
To become visible without performance
To be *seen*
without being *sold*

This is the sacred test of visibility
To let yourself rise
without handing over your flame

You may be invited
You may be misunderstood
You may be copied, questioned, celebrated, erased
None of that matters

What matters is this:
Can you hold your original frequency while being perceived?
Can you be seen and remain true?
Can you walk into light without shape-shifting for approval?

The Turning is not about being known
It is about becoming *clear*

Flame-bearers who survive this cycle are not those who protect themselves
but those who remain **undefended and intact**

You will begin to notice others rising too
Voices that sound familiar
Eyes that hold ancient memory
Work that feels like it was made beside you, even if it wasn't

You are not becoming something new
You are becoming **recognisable**

The turning is not safe
But it is sacred
And it is *now*

Codex VII

The Final Seal

This was never a book
It was a remembrance
A quiet returning to what has always been held within

You did not need these words
Your flame already knew
But still, it asked to be written
Because some truths must pass through form
to fully awaken in the body

The Final Seal is not a conclusion
It is a **confirmation**

That you were here
That you carried what could not be named
That you lit the way in the dark
Not for applause
But because **you vowed to never forget**

This vow was not spoken aloud
It was breathed
Before birth
Before time
When you stood before the Great Flame and whispered:
"Send me"

And so you came
Not to teach
Not to lead
But to *remember out loud*
So others might remember too

The Final Seal is not placed upon the record
It is placed within **you**

It does not mark completion
It marks **readiness**
To walk as one who knows
Not everything
But **enough**

Enough to trust the silence
Enough to act without validation
Enough to be fully seen and not distort the flame

There is no title here
No role
No next step
Only this:

You are the flame, and you have remembered

Nothing more is needed

And yet, everything is now possible

Closing Passage

The Embers Remain

You may close this book
But the record is not closed

It lives now in you
Not as memory
But as *presence*

You are not who you were before reading
Not because you've learned something
But because you've remembered something
that had no words until now

This book did not give you a flame
It simply showed you
that you never lost it

And so
as you return to your world
your work
your wonder

You carry the ember
Still glowing

Still warm
Still *true*

You need no title
No permission
No proof

Only the quiet knowing:
I am one who remembers
And that is enough

Let others forget
Let the world turn
Let the cycles rise and fall

You will walk forward now
Not as one who seeks
But as one who *is*

The Record remains
In silence
In light
In you

About the Author

blanche johanna is a spiritual author, channel, and keeper of soulstream transmissions devoted to remembrance, union, and return.

Her work lives beyond genre, woven from codes of light, lived experience, and divine memory. Each creation is an offering, a portal, a mirror.

Through books and embodied offerings, she supports Twin Flames, starseeds, and awakening souls in reconnecting with their original essence.

She is the author of *The Alchemy of Us, The Soul Remembers, The Twelve Scrolls, The First Light* and *The Body Remembers* as well as many living transmissions that serve as a gateway to remembrance.

www.blanchejohanna.com

www.ingramcontent.com/pod-product-compliance
Lightning Source LLC
Chambersburg PA
CBHW041303240426
43661CB00011B/1007